Chakras

Everything you need to know about using your chakras, chakra healing, chakra meditation, chakra clearing, and much more!

Copyright 2015

Table Of Contents

Introduction 1

Chapter 1: History of the Chakras 2

Chapter 2: Root Chakra 4

Chapter 3: Sacral Chakra 8

Chapter 4: Solar Plexus Chakra 12

Chapter 5: Heart Chakra 15

Chapter 6: Throat Chakra 18

Chapter 7: Third Eye Chakra 20

Chapter 8: Crown Chakra 22

Conclusion 24

Introduction

I want to thank you and congratulate you for downloading the book, "Chakras".

This book contains helpful information about your chakras, and how you can use them!

There are 7 main chakras in the body, each with a particular purpose, or power. This book will explain to you how each chakra affects your body and spirit, and why it's vital to keep these chakras clear.

Many people will have blocked chakras, and they need to be continually worked on to maintain health and wellbeing.

You will soon discover how to clear and heal your chakras through a variety of methods. Some of the included techniques include yoga poses, exercises, food, colors, and scents.

Also included are detailed descriptions of the history of each chakra. This includes the chakras colors, symbols, and meanings.

With the help of this book you will learn what chakras are, why they are important, what each chakra does, and how to keep all of them healthy!

I hope this book is able to help you in discovering the power of your chakras, and in ultimately improving your life!

Thanks again for downloading this book, I hope you enjoy it!

Chapter 1:
History of the Chakras

You may have heard of the Chakras from watching Naruto and Avatar: The Last Airbender. In the Japanese anime Naruto, Chakras are portrayed as the "lifeblood essence of all life and magic". Chakras are more than just plot factors in TV shows and the like. They have thousands of years of culture and tradition backing them up.

The word chakra is derived from the Sanskrit "cakra" which means "wheel". This refers to the belief that these chakras are spinning wheels of light, and many also call them wheels of life. The first mention of the chakra ever recorded was in the Vedas which are texts of knowledge of the ancient Hindus. It was written sometime between 1,500 to 500 B.C. Some believe that these teachings related to the chakras originated from Aryan tradition. The connection between these two traditions may be seen with the colors of the rainbow. Each chakra has its distinct color that can also be seen in the rainbow. In Aryan culture, the rainbow is the bridge that connects Asgard and Misgard.

The concept of Chakras found its way to the Western culture sometime in the 18th century. It is believed that German physician Franz Anton Mesmer used "animal magnetism" to cure diseases. His theory, later coined as mesmerism, centers on his belief that a natural force invisible to the eye is exerted by animals and that this force has healing effects. Though he garnered a number of believers and followers, people from the scientific and community probably regarded him as somewhat of a cuckoo. Nowadays, mesmerism is more related to the concept of hypnotism which is a technique taken from Mesmer's animal magnetism. Nowadays, the belief in the seven chakras is prevalent all around the world and people perform meditations and practice different yoga techniques for the purpose of clearing these chakras.

Ever since the concept of chakras became popular, a large number of ancient studies and practices have incorporated them. Though the chakra system may be different from teacher to teacher and school to school, there remains to be five characteristics common to all:

1. Chakras form part of the body, along with the *nadis* (breath channels) and *vayus* (winds).

2. The Chakras are all found within the *sushumna* or central channel.

3. There are two side channels that cross the center channel.

4. The chakras each have a specific number of 'petals' or 'spokes'.

5. Each Chakra is associated with a particular mantra seed-syllable, and certain colors and deities.

There are seven chakras or energy centers located all over the body. These chakras are where energy flows through. When a chakra is blocked, this often leads to some form of illness or condition. Healing in more than one chakra should not be done simultaneously. You should realign one chakra first before proceeding with the others, if necessary.

Chapter 2: Root Chakra

The First Chakra, otherwise known as the Base or Root Chakra, is located at the base of the spine along the coccygeal region or tailbone area. The Root Chakra, also called *Muladhara* in Sanskrit, is a representation of one's foundation. This chakra is also responsible for the feeling of being grounded and secure and is related to instinct and survival. The Root Chakra governs sexuality (physical), stability (mental), sensuality (emotional), and sense of security (spiritual).

Chakras involve nadis, which are energy channels through which divine energy travels. In the Root Chakra, the three most important *nadis* (*ida, pingala* and *sushumna*) are separate. These three ducts or channels begin their ascent from the *root chakra* which allows the energies of the body like the *prana shako* (vital force) and *manas shako* (mental force) to flow through each body part. It also believed that there are seven other chakras below the Root Chakra. These seven include the *Atala, Vitala, Sutala, Talatala, Rasatala, Mahatala* and *Patala*.

The most common emotional issues that affect the Root Chakra are issues of survival. These include financial independence, money and food. Once these issues are threatened, a temporary imbalance may occur in the Root Chakra. This is manifested as fear, anxiety, depression, confusion, the feeling of being in danger or not safe, abandonment, being discouraged, and hopelessness. Generally, it may feel like you are "losing grip". It may also be felt physically as pain in the lower back and lack of energy while also manifesting as skin problems. With this knowledge, you need to act on such problems by letting go of your fears and believing that you can get a hold of your life. Believe that everything will turn out for the better and that you belong in the universe. Learning how to heal your Root Chakra will do this for you.

The color vibration of the Root Chakra is red. Red represents the awakening of the sleeping consciousness and is associated with action and danger. The main symbol of the Root Chakra is a red four-petal lotus while its other symbols include a cube or square, and inverted triangle. The cube or square symbolizes grounding, solidity, safety and security. The animal that represents this chakra is an elephant with seven trunks while the sound vibration is LAM, pronounced 'lum'. Other representations of the Root Chakra are: Dakini (Shakti), Earth (element), Black Tourmaline and Master Quartz (crystals), Patchouli and Loosestrife (essences), Yesod (Tree of Life), and Gabriel and Sandalphon (archangels).

As for the healing and clearing exercises, any kind of physical activity will benefit your Root Chakra, especially those that make you aware of your body. When we say physical activity, some suggested exercises are walking, running, dancing, martial arts, Tai Chi, and yoga. Kundalini Yoga is one practice that can help in opening up your lower spine. Simple activities such as gardening, sweeping the floor, washing the dishes and cleaning your car also help this chakra. Even Zen meditation may also help open up your Root Chakra. It is important, though, not to overdo things. Avoid getting too exhausted.

The simplest exercise to heal you Root Chakra is to stomp your bare feet on the ground to make you feel grounded. Another way is to sink your weight downward. First, stand straight and relax your body. Separate your feet shoulder width apart. Bend your knees slightly then move your pelvis slightly forward. You need to keep your body balanced so your weight is distributed equally through your soles. Maintain this position for a number of minutes. You can also stimulate your *muladhara* by contracting your bottom muscles particularly your anus and genitals. While sitting down, or even standing up or walking, contract your muscles inward. Do this while inhaling. Relax these muscles when you exhale.

Doing the bridge pose is another way to heal your *muladhara*. To do this yoga pose, lie flat on your back with your knees bent. Keep your feet apart, hip wide with your toes pointing forward. Your arms and hands should be flat on the floor and at your sides. Then lift your hips while you exhale by pressing your weight into your feet. Your feet, arms and hands should stay flat on the ground. Make sure you don't flex your buttocks. Then interlock your hands and fingers just under your pelvis by rolling your shoulders back and extending your arms slowly. Slowly press your clasped hands onto the mat to lift your hips higher. Tuck the chin into the chest while moving the buttocks towards the knees then stretch your body as much as you can to lift higher. Remember to keep your weigh evenly distributed on all corners of your feet. After a minute, let go of your hands and place them flat, back on your sides. Slowly roll your spine back onto the floor while gradually exhaling.

There are other ways you can open and balance your Root Chakra. Practice doing the belly breathe or diaphragmatic breathing. When you are walking, do so with bare feet so you can be more grounded and closer to nature. Since red is the color vibration of the Root Chakra, you can wear pleasing shades of red. You can also light up some patchouli essential oil to surround yourself with its pleasing scent. Cedar and clove essential oils, as well as other earthy scents, will also do. Finally, you need to vocalize your affirmations. Keep reciting phrases such as, "Life is good", "I am safe", "I have all that I need" and other mantras that'll help you feel safe and grounded.

What you eat is also important to the health of your chakra. Mindfully consuming healthy food is important if you want your Root Chakra to stay open. The primary healing foods for the *muladhara* are red-colored foods like apples and beets and hot spices such as red cayenne peppers and Tabasco sauce. To stay grounded, you can also eat root vegetables like carrots and potatoes. Animal proteins such as red meat and eggs may also help as well as nuts and seeds.

Chapter 3:
Sacral Chakra

The Sacral Chakra is considered the seat of emotions and the second of the seven chakras. It is also known as *adhishthana*, *svadisthana* and *swadhisthana* which mean 'one's own abode'. This chakra is located in the sacrum, hence its name. The sacrum is the triangular bone near the base of the spine and at the top of the pelvic cavity. Focus on your lower abdomen particularly 2 inches below the navel then imagine going 2 inches further in, this is where the Sacral Chakra is supposed to be.

The *swadhisthana* also corresponds with the sex organs, particularly the testes and ovaries where sex hormones are produced. As such, the key issues of this chakra are basic emotional needs, addiction, relationships, pleasure and violence. The Sacral Chakra is also concerned with our creativity, connection, and ability to accept new experiences and other people. The emotional issues that usually affect the *swadhisthana* are pleasure, sexuality, well-being, and the sense of abundance. The Sacral Charka governs reproduction (physical), creativity (mental), joy (emotional), and enthusiasm (spiritual).

The Sacral Chakra receives universal force from the Root Chakra after the latter is done filtering the energy. Once the universal energy is received by the Sacral Chakra, it is turned into manifesting energy. This energy is like a magnet that attracts reality, which is a reflection of the thoughts and emotions in the chakra.

The Sacral Chakra has a color vibration of orange and is symbolized by a black lotus with six vermilion or orange petals. The petals represent affection, delusion, disdain, a feeling of all-destructiveness, pitilessness and suspicion. Inside the lotus is a crescent moon created by two circles. The crescent moon symbolizes the water region which is presided over by Varuna, the chakra's deity for material element. Its seed mantra or sound vibration is VAM and is represented by the crocodile of Varuna.

When the Second Chakra is balanced, you will come off as someone who radiates warmth, is extremely friendly, compassionate, emotionally stable, and energetic. Those with imbalanced or blocked *swadhisthana* are more likely to have attachment and trust issues. They may also be emotionally volatile, too sensitive, and suffer from guilt brought about by sexual history.

The main method of re-establishing balance in the Sacral Chakra is to physically root your pelvic floor into the Earth. In Kundalani yoga, the contraction of the genitals (*vajroli* mudra) and anus *(ashvini mudra)* are the main practices that help balance the Sacral Chakra. The Kegel exercise, though not a yoga practice, also helps since it stretches the muscles surrounding the female genitalia and the base of the penis. It also works out the muscles of the anus and the pubococcygeus or PC muscle.

There also specific yoga postures that allow you to open your hips. You need to let go of the physical and emotional tension in your hips and allow your reproductive organs to be restored. The following yoga postures will help you do that, but first, you need to meditate to help relax your mind and body

The *Tarasana* or Star Pose is done by sitting on the floor with your soles together. Drop your knees open to each side and keep your feet about two feet from your pelvic floor. Bend your body forward then place your hands on your feet. As you inhale, let your spine stretch. Exhaling longer, slowly roll your body forward until your forehead is on or near your heels. Hold this position for up to five minutes.

The Cobra Pose or *Bhujangasana* is not only a useful posture for the Sacral Chakra but also for the Third and Fourth Chakras which will be discussed later in the book. Just lie down on the floor with your palms and top of your feet flat. Tilt your pelvis and draw your belly button toward your spine to engage your abs. This will keep your lower back safe. Then bend your elbows and place your hands on your side getting ready to push. Press your palms into the floor while rotating the shoulders back and away from the ears. Slowly lift your upper body with your arms keeping your head and neck straight before tilting your chin upward. Your hips, legs and feet should remain flat on the floor. Stay in this position for five bull breaths before you release and return to the starting position.

The frog pose, otherwise called *mandukasana*, also is helpful in opening the Sacral Chakra. Go down on your arms and knees. Your knees should be at right angles while your arms are flat on the floor, parallel to your body, and pointing forward. Gently spread your legs, sliding your knees to each side. Your heels and pelvis should remain aligned with your knees. At this point, some of you may feel a little discomfort. If you are still able, spread your aligned knees and heels further. You can let your stomach rest on the floor if you can reach it. Stay in this position for up to five minutes, then slowly let your hands crawl forward to release.

Aside from the physical exercises, you also need to take charge of your emotions if you wish to keep your Sacral Chakra balanced. You have to learn how to let go of the emotions that make you unhappy and unhealthy. In other words, check your baggage by the door and carry on without all the weight that is pulling you down. Since the second Chakra is related to sexuality, you need to let go of your attachment to your past romantic and sexual relationships, including instances of miscarriages, abortions and infertility. Especially those who have suffered from sexual abuse will need to work on releasing pent up emotions.

As for this chakra's healing foods, go for orange-colored ones. Oranges, tangerines, and carrots are the first ones that come to mind. Any kind of seeds and nuts are also good for your Sacral Chakra. You can also have fats, oils, wild-caught salmon, and tropical fruits.

Chapter 4:
Solar Plexus Chakra

Also called *Manipura* or *Manipuraka*, the Solar Plexus Chakra is the third of the seven primary chakras. The *Manipura*, which translates to "resplendent gem", is located between the navel and the base of the sternum where the solar plexus and the digestive system are.

The Third Chakra is associated with the digestive and metabolic systems of the body. The Solar Plexus Chakra contains energy that is burning and transformative. This 'warrior' energy emits the essence of the self towards the outside world, which synchronizes the internal and external environments. The *Manipura* is also involved in self-esteem and the power to transform. It governs digestion (physical), expansiveness (emotion), personal power (mental), and growth (spiritual).

It is important to keep the Solar Plexus Chakra healthy in order to have a balanced flow of energy. This contributes to your ability to assert yourself, take risks, and accept responsibility for your own life. In other words, it helps you to assume power over your life with the help of better views of different life situations. The *Manipura* is responsible for the ability to be confident and to be in control of your life.

Manipura is symbolized by lotus with ten petals and a triangle pointing downward while the representing color of the Solar Plexus Chakra is yellow. The main element is fire which causes the purification of the past and boosts mental and spiritual awareness. The deity for material element is Agni while the presiding deity is Braddha Rudra and Lakini is its Shakti. The sound vibration or seed syllable is RAM.

The Cobra Pose is an effective posture to help open the Solar Plexus Chakra. Other yoga poses specifically aimed at this chakra are the Bow Pose, Crocodile Pose, Sealing Posture and leg lifts. *Dhanurasana* or Bow is done by lying on your stomach with the arms on the sides and the feet separated hip-width apart. Next, bend your knees up and reach your hands behind you to hold the ankles. Inhale while lifting your chest while pulling your legs up and back. Your body should be curved comfortably. Do not overstretch your spine. At this point, you resemble a bow, hence the name of this yoga pose. Stare directly in front of you and hold this position for 15 to 20 seconds. During these few seconds, don't forget to breathe deeply. Afterwards, exhale slowly as you release and return to the original position.

To do the Crocodile Pose, or *Nakra-Kriyas*, lie flat on your stomach with your arms and palms flat in front of you and the elbows slightly bent so your upper body is up. Open your legs and point your toes out to the sides. Your buttocks should be squeezed together while you're pressing on to the floor. Next, bend your elbows inward so that each palm is touching each forearm. Lift your chest while doing this. Finally, tuck your chin in and place your forehead on your arms. Breathe deeply while you are in this position. Exhale while releasing.

Sealing Posture or *Vajroli Mudra* works the urinary and reproductive systems along with the abdominal area including the solar plexus, which makes it helpful in opening both the Sacral and Solar Plexus Chakras. Before anything else, you need to have strong abdominal muscles. Do crunches or sit-ups to prepare your body for the *Vajroli Mudra*. Lie on your back with your palms flat on the floor and by your sides. Make sure your head, spine and legs are aligned. Inhale deeply and, as you breathe out, use your abdominals to lift your upper torso and your legs at the same time. Stay like this for a few seconds then inhale and release. Do around five repetitions.

Like the *Vajroli Mudra*, leg lifts both help open and balance the Second and Third Chakras. The first step in doing *Ardha Pada Hastasana*, (leg lifts), is to sit on the floor with your back straight. The legs should be stretched out in front. Place your palms on your knees and deeply breathe in then out. Lean forward so your forehead touches your knees. Hold your left foot with your left hand and then, while inhaling, lift your upper body along with your left arm and leg. Exhale slowly as you release and let your body come down. Do the same process with your right arm and leg.

To help heal your Solar Plexus Chakra, load up on complex carbohydrates, fiber, legumes, whole grain foods, and yellow-colored foods like corn, yellow lentils, and yellow sweet peppers. You can also surround yourself with the scents of grapefruit, rosemary, and orange essential oils, and wear gold jewelries and others with amber, topaz and other yellow gemstones. It is also vital to spend some time under the sun to absorb its yellow energy. You can also help by bringing back an old hobby, to reignite your lost curiosities and interests.

Chapter 5:
Heart Chakra

The Fourth Chakra is known as *Anahata-puri, Padmasundara, or Anahata,* which translates to "unhurt, unstruck and unbeaten". In simpler terms, it is the Heart Chakra. It is located at the center of the chest slightly above the heart. It is connected to the heart, thymus, lower lung and the circulatory system.

The Heart Chakra represents man's ability to love. That includes past and future loves. The emotional and mental issues related to the *Anahata* are love, confidence, equilibrium, inner peace, inspiration, joy, well-being, anger, fear, hate, jealousy, rejection, and other complex emotions. It is the force or energy that allows us to feel love, empathy, compassion and selflessness. It governs circulation (physical), unconditional love (emotion), passion (mental), and devotion (spiritual).

The symbol of *Anahata* is the heartmind, a circular greyish lotus flower with twelve petals. A *shatkona* or hexagram, formed by a yantra of two intersecting trangles, is found inside the heartmind. The hexagram represents the unification of man and woman. Green is its vibrating color while the seed mantra is YAM. It is also represented by emerald, malachite and rose quartz as its gemstones. The flower essences are California wild rose, holly and poppy. The presiding deity is Rudra Shiva while the Shakti is Kakini. Its element deity is the four-armed Vāyu, who rides an antelope, the chakra's animal representation.

An unbalanced or blocked Heart Chakra is manifested through being undisciplined, having relationship problems, and the dependence on another person to feel happiness. Events such as abandonment, adultery, heartbreak, separation, death, and emotional abuse affect the *Anahata*. Its physical manifestations include asthma, caber of the breast and lungs, pneumonia, shoulder issues, and heart problems.

To heal the Heart Chakra, the first thing you can do is to open your heart to love again, particularly, to love yourself. You can also perform different yoga poses to help the healing process.

The Camel Pose or *Ustrasana* opens the chest along with the Heart Chakra. Kneel on the floor making sure your knees are apart hip width apart, and your shins and top of the feet are pressed into the floor. Turn your thighs, which are perpendicular to the floor to start with, slightly inward to isolate the hip flexor. Narrow your hip points and squeeze your buttocks slightly. Make sure your hips and buttocks are not rigid. Place your palms flat, fingers pointing downward, on the back of your pelvis with the bases on the top of your buttocks. Lengthen your lower back while doing a pelvic tilt. Inhale, then roll the shoulders back while bending your body back to make an arch. Let your chest expand and keep your pelvis forward. You may feel a little uncomfortable at this point. If your hips and knees become a bit stiff, stop for a while to let your body become accustomed. Then gently twist to one side so you can put your hand on the back of the heel on the same side. Go back to the center and do the same with the other hand and heel. Press your thighs forward carefully to keep them perpendicular to your knees. If your back is feeling strained, contain your bottom front ribs and carry the hip points towards said ribs. You can either let your neck float back or keep staring forward so your head is straight as well. If your neck is bent back, keep your throat relaxed by opening your mouth. Hold your breath and stay in this position for twenty to sixty seconds. Contract your stomach muscles as you exhale and gradually put your hands, one by one, on the back of your pelvis. Upon inhaling, contract your abdominals once more to lift your chest forward making sure your neck is not strained.

To balance your chakra through the Fish Pose or *Matsyasana*, the first step is to lie on your back with the knees bent and your feet flat on the floor. As you take in air, lift your pelvis and slide your hands under your buttocks. The palms should be flat on the floor as you sit on them. Inhale once more while pressing your forearms and elbows on the mat. Slowly lift your upper body and head, then relax your head back to the floor. This will make your spine curve and create an arch. Hold for 15 to 30 seconds before releasing while exhaling slowly.

The breathing technique called *Sukh-Purkav* should be practiced at least thrice in the morning and again before going to bed so you can fully take advantage of its benefits to your body, especially the Heart Chakra. As you go along, you can increase the number of times you practice this breathing technique. You begin by closing your right nostril using your right thumb. Count three 'oms' as you inhale gradually through the other nostril. Then close your left nostril with your right hand and hold your breath while counting six or twelve 'oms'. You should be allowing a current to flow through your spine down to your tailbone and imagining that this current reaches the chakra, waking up the Kundalini. Next, exhale through the right nostril with a count of six 'oms'. Repeat the procedure this time starting with your left nostril. After each round, lie down for a while to relax your breathing and your body.

To further balance your chakra, feast on green-colored foods like leafy vegetables and green tea while inhaling holly and poppy scents. Wearing green clothing will also help.

Chapter 6:
Throat Chakra

The Fifth Chakra known as *Vishuddha* or *Vishuddhi* is more commonly called the Throat Chakra. It is located at the throat, obviously, but is also related to our ears and mouth. It is connected to the thyroid gland, where thyroid hormone is produced. This hormone aids in growth and maturity. This chakra governs communication (physical), fluent thought (mental), independence (emotional), and sense of security (spiritual).

The Throat Chakra is related to our ability to communicate or express ourselves, which includes speaking and hearing. Among its emotional issues are self-expression of feelings, and the truth.

Its main symbol is a white flower with sixteen purple petals. Inside it is a triangle pointing downward with a full moon inside it as well. The chakra is represented by the deity Ambara who is known to have four arms with a goad and a noose in them. He sits on a white elephant, the *Vishudda*'s representing animal. The material element is aether or akasha. The sound syllable is HAM while its colors are aquamarine and blue.

An unhealthy Throat Chakra is manifested through poor learning ability, difficulty in expressing oneself, fear, lying, uncertainty, and ultimately decay and death. Opening and balancing this chakra is concerned with yoga poses and other practices that focus on the throat.

Sarvangasana or Shoulder Stand has many variations. One way to do it is by lying down on your back, legs together and straight, arms on your side and palms flat on the floor. Press your hands on the floor, then breathe in and lift your legs as you exhale. Keep your knees straight. Place your hands on your back with the elbows as close to each other as possible. Once the legs are up, tuck your chin and do slow belly breathes. Stay in this position as long as it is comfortable.

To engage the Throat Lock or *Jalandhara Bandha*, sit comfortably with your legs crossed. Breathe in about two-thirds full of your lungs then hold your breath. Tuck your chin close to your chest and hold as long as comfortable then raise your chin and exhale.

Other ways of unblocking the Throat Chakra is through meditation, singing, chanting and playing a musical instrument. Consuming different kinds of fruits, sauces, sea plants, soups, teas and juices also help to heal this chakra.

Chapter 7:
Third Eye Chakra

The Third Eye Chakra is the sixth of the seven main chakras. *Ajna* which translates as 'command' is situated between the eyes and behind the forehead or where the 'third eye' is supposed to be.

The Third Chakra is directly associated with the senses of sight and hearing. It is also deemed the eye of intellect and intuition, and the seat of understanding. This means that it provides the ability to think clearly and make decisions. In other words, this chakra is responsible for how we perceive things around us. Its other emotional issues are imagination, intuition and wisdom. It is also responsible for the proper function and production of hormones.

The main representation of the Third Eye Chakra is a white flower with two white petals (dedicated to the sun and moon), and a white moon inside. This moon, which depicts the Shakti Hakini, has six faces and arms holding a book, drum, rosary and a skull. The seed syllable is AUM or "Pravana Om" while its color is indigo or violet.

Manifestations of an unbalanced or blocked *Anja* are confusion, indecision, jumping to conclusions, and inability to focus. To heal the chakra, you need to stimulate it.

Trataka or steady gazing is one way of stimulating your Third Eye Chakra. This practice is rather simple. Just focus your attention on a single tiny object. You can use a candle flame or a tiny black dot. While staring, you should pay attention to any thought and feeling that comes, and simply let them go. Continue doing this until your eyes become watery and instinctively close. Focus on the image that you can 'see' after closing your eyes. Use your third eye to keep the image there.

One yoga pose you can do to clear the Third Eye Chakra is the Fish Pose or *Matsyasana* which was already described in the sixth chapter.

The healing foods for this chakra are purple-red foods such as blackberries, grapes, and red onions. Chocolate, caffeine, tea and spices will also help.

Chapter 8:
Crown Chakra

The seventh and last chakra is the Crown Chakra. It is known as *Sahasrara* in Sanskrit, which translates to '1000-petalled lotus'. It is located near the top or crown of the head and is related to the brain, pituitary and pineal glands, and the central nervous system.

The Crown Chakra is associated with the state of pure or higher consciousness, along with detachment from illusion, inner wisdom and death of the body. It is believed that one who succeeds in attaining pure consciousness by raising the *kundalini* up to this chakra, *Nirvikalpa* (being one with God) is attained. In simpler terms, the Crown Chakra is related to our ability to be spiritually connected. Among its emotional issues are pure bliss and inner and outer beauty.

Its main symbol is a lotus with a thousand petals of different colors, arranged in twenty layers. At the center is a circular moon with a downward triangle. The chakra colors are lavender and pastel colors.

When the *Sahasrara* is healthy, it is manifested as confidence in their faith in a higher entity or force. When it is out of balance, it may be physically manifested as clumsiness, incoordination, and imbalance, while also showing up as a lack of spiritual exploration.

Some ways to open this chakra are cardio exercises like running, and meditation. As for yoga poses, you can do *Matsyasana* and *Sukh-Purkav* (see Chapter 6) as well as *Sarvangasana* (see Chapter 7). Healing this chakra can't be achieved through food, unlike the other six chakras. The

Crown Chakra is 'fed' with forces related to the spirit such as clean and fresh air, sunlight, and love.

Conclusion

Thank you again for downloading this book!

I hope this book was able to help you learn more about chakras, and how you can use them.

Healing your chakras is essential for enlightenment, health, and overall wellbeing. If you are stuck with any of the yoga pose descriptions, there are a range of tutorial videos available on YouTube.

Good luck with healing your chakras, and improving your wellbeing!

The next step is to put this information to use, and begin working on your own abilities!

Finally, if you enjoyed this book, please take the time to share your thoughts and post a review on Amazon. It'd be greatly appreciated!

Thank you and good luck!

www.ingramcontent.com/pod-product-compliance
Lightning Source LLC
LaVergne TN
LVHW021750060526
838200LV00052B/3557